Real Cats Don't Do Talk Shows

Mort Gerberg

PRICE/STERN/SLOAN
Publishers, Inc., Los Angeles
1983

ISBN: 0-8431-0747-2

FOR
LILIA and PIXEY

REAL CATS DO NOT HAVE
MANICURES OR PEDICURES
BY HEAVILY MASCARAED
LADIES IN PERFUMED
BEAUTY SALONS.

REAL CATS SHARPEN THEIR
OWN CLAWS ON THE
FURNITURE.

REAL CATS DO NOT
HAVE A CUP OF EXPRESSO
AND A CROISSANT FOR
BREAKFAST EVERY
MORNING.

**REAL CATS DO NOT TAKE
THEIR MODELING
PORTFOLIOS AROUND.**

REAL CATS ARE NOT BETTER
KNOWN THAN THE VICE
PRESIDENT OF THE UNITED
STATES.

REAL CATS DON'T
DO TALK SHOWS.

REAL CATS DO NOT HAVE
THOUGHT BALLOONS
FLOATING OVER THEIR
HEADS.

REAL CATS DON'T SNEER ON CUE.

REAL CATS DO *NOTHING* ON CUE.

REAL CATS HAVE LITTLE
USE FOR JANE FONDA'S
EXERCISE CLASSES.

REAL CATS DO NOT ATTEND
FANCY BUFFETS AND EAT
BROCCOLI IN CLAM DIP,
POACHED SALMON, MOUSE
MOUSSE OR SPINACH
QUICHE.

WHAT REAL CATS *DO* IS
STALK MICE, GOLDFISH,
BIRDS AND INSECTS, AND
KILL AND EAT THEM, IF
AT ALL POSSIBLE.

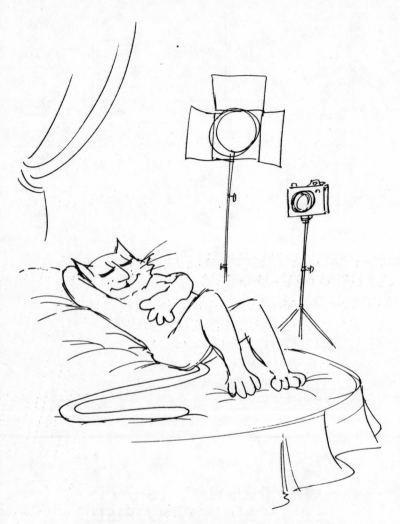

**REAL CATS DO NOT POSE
FOR CALENDARS . . .**

... REAL CATS COULDN'T
CARE LESS WHAT *DAY* IT IS
... OR WHAT *MONTH* ... OR
EVEN WHAT *YEAR*.

**REAL CATS ARE NOT
USUALLY KNOWN AS
FOUNTAINS OF WISDOM
AND TRUTH...**

... OR AS DISPENSERS OF
DEEP AND MEANINGFUL
PSYCHOLOGICAL INSIGHTS
FOR THE MIND ...

. . . OR SOUL.

REAL CATS, IN POINT OF
FACT, DO NOT REALLY
RELATE WELL WITH ANY-
ONE ELSE—NOR DO THEY
CARE TO.

**REAL CATS DO NOT ATTEND
CHIC COCKTAIL PARTIES
AND ENGAGE YOU IN
CHIT CHAT.**

**WHAT REAL CATS *DO* IS
CROUCH UNDER CARS AND
PEER OUT FROM BEHIND
WHEELS AT YOU.**

**REAL CATS DO NOT OWN
ANSWERING MACHINES,
WITH OR WITHOUT REMOTE
BEEPERS.**

**REAL CATS WOULD BE
SATISFIED IF NOBODY
TELEPHONED THEM
IN THE FIRST PLACE.**

REAL CATS DO NOT GET IN
TOUCH WITH THEIR
FEELINGS.

REAL CATS DO NOT TAKE
EST, SENSITIVITY TRAINING
OR GESTALT THERAPY; NOR
DO THEY GO TO ASHRAMS
TO MEDITATE.

COMMUNICATION-WISE,
WHAT REAL CATS *DO* IS
LIE AROUND LOOKING
INSCRUTABLE...

. . . OR SIT ON
FENCES AT NIGHT,
YOWLING .

IF A REAL CAT *HAD* TO HAVE A JOB, HE'D BE A FREE-LANCER. A REAL CAT WOULD *NEVER* WORK FOR ANYONE ELSE.

REAL CATS DO NOT WEAR
DESIGNER SCARVES FROM
BLOOMINGDALE'S OR
NEIMAN MARCUS...

REAL CATS DON'T WEAR
DESIGNER *ANYTHING*.
REAL CATS GO AROUND
BARE-CLAWED.

REAL CATS DO NOT NUMBER
DOGS AMONG THEIR BEST
BUDDIES.

REAL CATS DO NOT READ
"THE JOY OF SEX" OR GUIDES
TO LOVEMAKING BY HELEN
GURLEY BROWN . . .

. . . NOR DO THEY FREQUENT
PORNO SHOPS OR X-RATED
MOVIES .

REAL CATS REALLY *DO* IT—
LOUD AND CLEAR.

REAL CATS DO NOT PLAY
BACKGAMMON, SOLVE
RUBIK'S CUBES OR WORK
DOUBLE CROSTIC PUZZLES.

**REAL CATS DO NOT TAKE
TENNIS LESSONS.**

REAL CATS DO NOT HAVE A
SUBSCRIPTION SERIES TO
THE OPERA.

REAL CATS AMUSE THEM-
SELVES—WITH MOTHS, SUN-
BEAMS AND DRIPPING
WATER.

REAL CATS DON'T JOG IN
FANCY ADIDAS OUTFITS TO
STAY IN GOOD SHAPE . . .

REAL CATS ARE *ALWAYS* IN
GOOD SHAPE.

REAL CATS DON'T BRUSH
THEIR TEETH AFTER EVERY
MEAL, MASSAGE THEIR
GUMS, USE A WATER PIK,
DENTAL FLOSS AND AN
ASTRINGENT MOUTHWASH.

REAL CATS EAT CRUNCHIES.

CRUNCH
EASE

REAL CATS DO NOT RIDE UNICYCLES ON TIGHTROPE WIRES, JUGGLE FLAMING TORCHES, ROLLER SKATE IN TUBS OF RASPBERRY JELL-O, OR DO *ANYTHING* TO AMUSE OTHERS.

**REAL CATS DO NOT USE
ELEVATORS OR ESCALATORS.**

REAL CATS *CLIMB*.

REAL CATS DON'T GET
ADDICTED TO PAC-MAN,
FROGGER, SPACE INVADERS
OR OTHER ELECTRONIC
HOME ENTERTAINMENT.

REAL CATS ARE SATISFIED
WITH THE WARMTH OF THE
TELEVISION SET.

REAL CATS WOULD NEVER
SERVE IN THE ARMY.

REAL CATS JUST DON'T
TAKE ORDERS.

REAL CATS DON'T NEED
SLEEPING PILLS, EYE SHADES
OR EAR PLUGS TO HELP
THEM FALL ASLEEP.

REAL CATS DON'T DRINK
SKIM OR LOW FAT MILK.

IF THEY DRINK IT AT *ALL*,
REAL CATS DRINK *WHOLE*
MILK.

REAL CATS DON'T LIKE
PAPERBACKS.

REAL CATS ONLY LIKE
BOOKS IN HARDCOVER.

IF IT WERE UP TO THEM,
REAL CATS WOULD NEVER
EVEN GO *NEAR* A CAT SHOW,
LET ALONE *PARTICIPATE*
IN ONE.

REAL CATS DO NOT DO
TV COMMERICALS FOR
AMERICAN EXPRESS.

REAL CATS DON'T TAKE
MEETINGS.

REAL CATS DO NOT SING
ITALIAN OPERA IN THE
BATH.

THE ONLY THING A REAL
CAT HATES MORE THAN
OPERA IS BEING IMMERSED
IN WATER.

REAL CATS DON'T TAKE
FOREIGN LANGUAGE
LESSONS AT BERLITZ.

WHAT A REAL CAT *DOES* IS SAY "MEOW" AND PURR, AND THAT'S *IT*.

**REAL CATS DO NOT WAIT
AROUND FOR SOMEBODY TO
GIVE THEM A HANDOUT.**

WHAT REAL CATS *DO* IS SCROUNGE AROUND FOR THEMSELVES.

REAL CATS DO NOT BELIEVE
IN REINCARNATION, THAT
THEY ARE MEDIUMS FOR
COMMUNICATING WITH
SPIRITS, OR THAT THEY
HAVE NINE LIVES.

WHAT REAL CATS *DO*
BELIEVE IN IS *ONE* LIFE, TO
BE ENJOYED BY GETTING
THEIR BELLIES SCRATCHED,
RUBBING UP AGAINST YOUR
LEG OR SNOOZING IN
THE SUN.

REAL CATS DON'T WEAR GLASSES—EVEN FOR READING.

REAL CATS DON'T GET
KILLED BY CURIOSITY.

**REAL CATS DON'T MAKE
HOME MOVIES OR TAPES TO
PRESERVE PRECIOUS
MOMENTS FOR MEMORY.**

**REAL CATS LIVE ONLY IN
THE PRESENT TENSE.**